Paint the Sky

Kristin Martin

Paint the Sky

For David, Che and Matt
with love

and
for Mum
I miss you

Paint the Sky
ISBN 978 1 76041 258 6
Copyright © text Kristin Martin 2016
Cover photo: Shannon Mowling

First published 2016 by
Ginninderra Press
PO Box 3461 Port Adelaide 5015 Australia
www.ginninderrapress.com.au

Contents

Love Shared	7
Mum	9
Caress	10
Six Times Round the Sun	11
Jason and Rochelle	12
Time and Space	14
I Thought I Knew Her	16
Darling	17
Grey-tinted Glasses	18
It's Work	19
The Catch of the Evening	20
His Lament	21
Sweetest Failure	22
Till Death Do Us	23
Four People in One Day	24
Mary at 96	25
Mother Earth	27
A Sonnet for Mother Earth	29
Whistling Kites	30
En Route	31
Memories by the Murray	32
The Waves	34
Never Happy with the Weather	35
The Parties	36
Beyond the Dingo Fence	38
Inspired Hope	39
A Walk by the Sea	40
The Threat of Genetics	41
The Leaky Tap Swamp	42
Belonging	44

Well Past Midnight — 45

- Wading — 47
- My mind — 48
- A Bark of Thunder — 49
- Traitorous Eyes — 50
- In the Back of Emily Dickinson — 52
- His Hand — 54
- A(n end of) Love Sonnet — 55
- Sleeping Rough — 56
- The Shed — 57
- The Four of Us — 58
- The Power of a Pen — 60
- Jealousy — 61
- My Dearest Love — 62
- I slip — 63

Waves of Grief — 65

- Snowflakes on Your Coffin — 67
- The Night Before Her Funeral — 68
- After — 69
- You Think — 70
- Grandma's Grey Goggles — 71
- Waves of Grief — 74
- Today — 75
- Left Baggage — 76
- Last Night — 77
- She Paints the Sky — 78
- Simple — 79

Acknowledgements — 80

Love Shared

The parents, from their fireside place,
Behold that pleasant scene,
And joy is on the mother's face,
Pride, in the father's mien.

– Charlotte Bronte

Mum

There.
That gesture.
When I brushed the back of my fingers
across my son's fevered cheek.
That was yours.
As were the quiet words I soothed him with.
Even my name,
that he called in the too-early morning,
pulling me from my bed to his side,
as you did with me, so many times,
that too
I took from you.

Caress

Their arms entwined in newfound bliss,
their skin aflame with passion's kiss,
her eyes lift from his tight clasped hand
to watch the waves caress the sand.

His small pink feet run to the sea,
she races after anxiously
and holds him squirming on the land
to watch the waves caress the sand.

With yaps and growls he taunts the waves
then runs back to the hand he craves.
She calms him with her fingers spanned
to watch the waves caress the sand.

With leathered arms, still brown and strong,
he safely pushes her along.
She smiles as he helps her stand
to watch the waves caress the sand.

The ocean shows its gentle side
to draw its viewers to its tide.
In loving pairs they sit or stand
to watch the waves caress the sand.

Six Times Round the Sun

He's been round the sun six times,
back and forth between the stars,
journeyed deep into the Mesozoic
and onwards to the unknown.
Yet here he is,
chin on my shoulder,
knees digging into my belly,
like there's nothing in his world
except us.

Jason and Rochelle

The University Bar was two-thirds empty, the quietest Jason had seen it all year.
Rochelle found it unpleasantly crowded.

She was drawn to his confidence and the comfort his degree promised.
He fell in love with her hair.

Their first flat was chosen for its location, the other side of town from his parents,
two streets from hers.

The salon needed painting and the customers expected her to talk but at least it paid the rent.
He promised when he finished the doctorate she'd never work again.

He enjoyed the stimulation of his studies.
She took pleasure in the quiet mornings before he rose

and learned to spend the evenings in her mother's kitchen.
He learned he could always watch what he liked on TV.

Before long he discovered that her personality was as lifeless as her long bleached strands,
while she'd already realised that his confidence was just a ruse for getting his own way.

But by then there were the twins, Mary-Jane, after her great-aunts
and, the pride of his life, Albert.

His first job paid five times as much as hers, not counting the relocation expenses.
She hoped the compound would be full of friendly mothers and young kids.

It wasn't,
but there were plenty of young attractive housewives willing to stray.

Still, he preferred his second job in Canada as it was safer and not as hot.
She initially agreed, but soon grew to hate the cold.

The second winter she took the kids to her mother's.
He went to court and made her bring them back.

The week-on, week-off parenting suited his work commitments.
She had trouble finding things to fill her days.

But at least she still had the kids. And her hair.
He took up golf and became president of the social club.

Jason's new wife stood up to him and he learnt to enjoy her choice of TV shows.
Rochelle never stopped missing her mother.

Time and Space

Vein-streaked hands
tucked out of sight,
she leans forward,
head tilted just so,
in that position
long perfected
to elicit disclosure.

He's all
knees and elbows
as he gazes,
anywhere but at her eyes,
eager words tumbling
to explain his obsession.

So Gran…
She stifles a flinch.
The name that conjures love
and pain
in equal parts.

…since the dawn of time…
She hears,
remembering her dawn,
all that youthful vigour.

…the Universe…
She sighs.
For her the World
was enough.

…has been expanding…
She knows too well.
Unfamiliar spaces,
strange contraptions.

And it's still expanding!
Can you imagine the distance?
And she thinks
she almost can.
About as far as the lavatory
at 3 a.m.

I Thought I Knew Her

We'd worked together for half a year,
graduated from a polite *how was your weekend?*
to accepting each other's advice about our kids.

That day I'd entered the lunchroom with my mind at my desk
when I was grabbed by the silence,
the usual clutter of chatter replaced by one voice.

I saw her tension
and that sideways neck tilt she does when she's thinking
before I processed her words.

Dad was killed. My younger brothers too.
Mum died on my arm. I was nine.
Pol Pot, you know?

And in the jumble of my thoughts were
how could you survive that? and raise a family? and go to
    work? and live your life like anything matters?

And how could I not know?

Darling

Have you brushed your teeth, Darling?
silence
That was a question. Questions need answers.
silence, with the occasional click of Lego
I would like to know if you've brushed your teeth.
silence, with the occasional click of Lego and the emergence of a structure
Darling, do I need to go get your toothbrush for you or have you already brushed your teeth?
silence, with the occasional click of Lego and the emergence of a structure that is amazingly complicated
Darling?
silence, with the occasional click of Lego and the emergence of a structure that is amazingly complicated and why on Earth do I even bother talking when all that is going on in his head and nothing I say is ever going to get through to him
Darling, can I have a cuddle?
silence as two small arms engulf me

Grey-tinted Glasses

He never could find the rose-tinted glasses.
When he looked back on his life
all too often it was a grey-tinted pair that settled
onto the bridge of his broad nose;
showing the rouging embarrassments,
repeating the words he wished he'd said but never had the
    courage,
magnifying the inadequate summers and lonely winters
but never bringing forth the belly laughs
or the love he'd shared with his child
or simply the joy he'd felt
when picking his tomatoes.

It's Work

Her darling leaves her side, runs ahead into the classroom.
Already the rumours swirl and grow.

Where's the teacher?
Had a crash. Went to hospital in an ambulance.

But, as is her way,
she sifts out the truth.

Darling, the teacher's late
because she got stuck behind an accident.

She smiles and kisses his cheek,
while inside she's building up her barrier.

Perched on the low chair she listens to him read, encouraging,
not letting on that his words aren't reaching her.

When her phone rings
she takes it quietly.

Sorry, Darling, it's work,
I gotta go.

She kisses him goodbye,
heads off to don her uniform

and inform another mother
that her darling's gone.

The Catch of the Evening

When the gully breeze bustled through the gums
skimming the heat from the day
we bowled out of the house
and set up stumps under the blue gum.
As always, the catches were what mattered.
Mum's was the first.
She glanced up from yanking a thistle out of the hardened pitch
and plucked the ball from the air.
Jack caught me out on the full
ball clasped tight against his chest
his whoops and air punches claiming more skill than he displayed.
Dad didn't even get a look-in
with his collection of one-hand-one-bounces
but I caught him mid-air with a spectacular leap from atop the slide.
Then, as the mosquitos herded us indoors,
I turned to grab the stumps and saw the uncontested winner:
our blue gum. It had caught the moon
and was holding it triumphantly
in the crook of a branch.

His Lament

His lament is my desire,
those two words uttered
with a seven-year-old's contempt
no longer piercing my armour
but sliding like butter down the hardened steel.

As I labour to conquer tasks
and tether thoughts that scatter the moment I pursue another
I find a trickle of memory
when time was a freshly mown field with fences beyond my imagination
and a forgotten self uttered those words he now claims as his own:
I'm bored.

Sweetest Failure

from the first flutter
I knew
the first smile
he knew
that she was our joy beyond measure

from our single
mistake
of misjudging my
rhythm
we created our exquisite treasure

Till Death Do Us

With foundations forged on fragile ground,
differing by more than a degree,
her nest ties strong, his barely there,
but still that need to prove to them,
they built their life and added more.

Then came the lure of safer soil.
They lifted their feeble structure,
deposited it on foreign dirt,
and watched it crumble.

His parting caused her but a tremor.
What levelled her,
shook her breathless to the earth,
were the iron rods with which he clasped their children.

She could not sink supports in this strange soil,
nor return to her nest alone.
So she sits through each day in her structure-less shell
and dreams
   of his death.

Four People in One Day

He left work an educated man,
strode from the surgery in suited confidence,
oblivious to the gossiping girl behind the desk.

He arrived home a doting son,
shed shoes for quieter slippers,
his jacket for the shared warmth of central heating.

He knocked on her bedroom door a trembling boy,
alarmed by the too silent house,
apologies huddled on his lips.

He knelt beside her as all three:
his education noted the rigor mortis,
the son was crushed by guilt,
while the boy continued trembling.

He returned to work a dishevelled soul,
stumbling behind the girl's desk
to soak in the comfort of her words.

Mary at 96

She grew up in another time.
A time when doctors were rare
and loss of hearing through infection, common.
A time when fourteen was old enough for full-time work
but only till a girl was married.

Now, sitting in her favourite chair,
hearing aid in place, eyes sparkling,
she recounts how, after the wedding,
he insisted that she stop work,
and how, each day, she waited until he left,
and went anyway.

Mother Earth

Nature, the gentlest mother,
   Impatient of no child

   – Emily Dickinson

A Sonnet for Mother Earth

The passing years have proved unkind. Her pride,
the hair, which in her youth grew thick and dark,
its beauty matched by neither babe nor bride,
has thinned, and frequently her scalp shows stark.

Her skin, no longer the unblemished sheath,
peeks haggard, grey, from under dowdy garb,
while septic blood flows through her veins beneath
to spurt from wounds cut by a savage barb.

Her gentle breath's past sweetness lies forgot
as decades smoking leave it foul and warm.
In years she's far from young, but old she's not.
Her age does not deserve this ugly form.

Her only wish: to have the chance to heal.
Restore her beauty. End her cruel ordeal.

Whistling Kites

a collection of kites
dip and soar
through the too blue sky

their invisible strings held
by daredevil kids
standing unseen
on the red-fringed road

when a thoughtless road train
barrels through
strings snag, stretch and snap

their sport ruined
the kids tumble away

while the kites
with an exultant whistle
and a tilt of their wide brown wings
escape into the corners of the sky

En Route

At first, the water's calm
was a mockery.
The waves, with their illusion of gentleness,
sniggered behind azure fingers.

The ocean breeze kissed her cheek
with her grandmother's lips,
as if it too wished her good health
and prosperity.

But she was not fooled.
With bodies pressed in close,
she saw nothing but the endless sea,
felt nothing but her churning anxiety.

As the hours trickled past
the ocean grew to mimic her.
It roiled like her stomach,
roared like the explosions echoing endlessly in her mind.

When at last
the feeble craft capsized
the ocean's fingers, no longer blue,
clasped her tight.

Memories by the Murray

Do you recall that summer morning's breakfast by the billabong
when water birds enthralled us with their beauty and their lilting song?
The spoonbills skimmed the glass veneer in search of food between the reeds;
your spoon was frozen while you watched them scoop up fish beside the weeds.
The pelicans, those princely statues chiselled from the fallen tree,
infused us with a sense of awe that coloured all the scenery.

Do you recall that summer weekend in the stifling afternoon
when you and I plunged to our knees into the cool, serene lagoon?
The velvet mud caressed our feet, adorning them with silken veils
while fish swam near our outstretched hands obscured by their murky trails.
The gum trees beckoned from the islands advertising mottled shade.
We lay together peacefully beneath their dappled green brocade.

Do you recall that summer evening stretching far into the night
when we both paddled inky waters, candelabras for our light?
We listened to nocturnal calls of shadowed creatures seldom
 seen.
Our paddles added rhythmic beats to form a symphony
 serene.
The stars outshone our feeble candles, decorating night-time's
 sky.
We snuggled close and gazed above while endless hours
 drifted by.

Do you recall that dismal summer when the water
 disappeared?
And in its place evolved a mudflat from which precious life
 was seared.
The birds flew off to wetter lands and all the reeds were laid
 to dust.
The grand old gums shed heavy limbs upon the ugly
 hardened crust.
Our memories are what remain of that delightful billabong.
Let's hope for rain and beg for flow so it returns before too
 long.

The Waves

the waves rush onto the shore
they pound with ferocious might
his words come out in a roar
she pleads with him not to fight

they pound with ferocious might
grinding the rocks into sand
she pleads with him not to fight
she backs away from his hand

grinding the rocks into sand
they show their colossal force
she backs away from his hand
she's yelling, her voice is hoarse

they show their colossal force
they'd strip carcasses to bone
she's yelling, her voice is hoarse
she slips on a foam capped stone

they'd strip carcasses to bone
his words come out in a roar
she slips on a foam capped stone
the waves rush onto the shore

Never Happy with the Weather

Tired of the freezing air biting our toes and fingers
as we rush to dress,
and the mist that wraps our car on the morning drive
– so that we can't see the trees beside the road –
we pack our caravan and head north.

Past Uluru
through the desert
to the red hills of the Kimberley,
where the fat boab trees wave their wild arm-like branches,
and the gorges of broken orange rock stand stark against the clear blue sky.

As we drive down another endless red road
with the sweat dripping down our bellies,
the flies buzzing at the window
and the dust thick on our tongues,
a car overtakes us.

And we pretend that the cloud of dust that wraps our car
– so that we can't see the trees beside the road –
is lovely, freezing cold mist.

The Parties

On the morning of my eighth birthday
the storm had quietened.
The wind, after shouting itself hoarse in the night,
barely whispered through the trees,
while the sun smiled at me in spurts between grey clouds.

After birthday pancakes with Mum, Dad and Jess,
I'd unwrapped my presents on the lounge-room floor.
It's as bad as outside, Jess had sneered,
looking from the wrapping paper-strewn room
through the window to the branches littering our lawn.

Mum had laughed and ushered me back to the kitchen
where I'd helped her make the sausage rolls,
Just like Gran's,
and the speckled fairy bread,
Because you're never too old for fairy bread.

Then we'd set the table.
Six plates: orange, red, purple, blue, yellow and green,
a rainbow table ready for a party.
Your friends better not come in my room!
Jess had barked, and after I'd punched her one

Mum sent us outside to collect the windfall.
Jess had grabbed the basket and together
we'd skidded across the grass to the orange trees,
and ducked under the dripping canopy
to find the thick-skinned fruits.

We'd half-filled the basket when suddenly Jess squealed,
Ooh, yuck! *Rats*! and pointed under the curry bush.
They've stolen our oranges.
She backed away while I rushed in, peering under the low
    dense branches.
There were no rats in sight.

But my stab of disappointment was replaced by awe
at what was left of the oranges.
The sweet juicy fruit had been nibbled clean away
leaving six perfect bowls, laid out on the swept-dirt mat:
another table ready for a party.

Beyond the Dingo Fence

She's stretched out on her rock-hard bed,
head pillowed on her ample paws.
Her blanket is the morning sun –
as warm as wool but light as gauze.

She lifts her head as we approach
and stares at us with fearless eyes.
Her golden body blocks our path.
There's not the slightest sign she'll rise.

Dave hits the brakes and honks the horn.
Get off the road! I cry in fright.
She waits a heartbeat more, then stands,
pads off the road and out of sight.

Inspired Hope

Her silent anger fills the car
not diminishing with the distance.
At the campground he spies

a pale, smooth-skinned gum
growing beside a rough acacia,
their limbs entwined like lovers.

With inspired hope
he pitches the tent
beneath their shade.

After a meal eaten, but not shared,
they slink into separate sleeping bags.
She firmly turns her back.

Frog calls fill the night
expelling
his last dreams of sleep.

Withdrawing into the moonlight
he glares in envy
at the devotedly embracing trees.

A Walk by the Sea

I went for a walk
alone by the sea
but the water kept me company.

I whispered to it
as I walked on its sand
and told it of all the things I planned.

It whispered to me
as I walked on its shore
and told me secrets from long before.

I went for a walk
with my friend the sea
and we kept each other company.

The Threat of Genetics

History, and the threat of genetics,
set him on his daily trudge to the outlet
    and back
spurred on by his youngest sister's tactlessness,
    disguised as honesty,
when she announced as he blew out the candles
you're the age Dad was at the first of his three heart attacks
    and when was the last time you raised a sweat?

But as he defiantly pounded history into the sand
and pushed genetics back into the soupy sea
    scraps of pleasure surprised him.

The pink cockleshell mirrored in the morning sky.
    The comic pelican perched atop its statue.
        The rippled tide pool capturing cotton-wool clouds.

He gradually grew to realise it was the highlight of his day,
    and though he would never put it into words,
he felt thankful for his sister's lack of tact.

The Leaky Tap Swamp

on the edge of a dry trampled field
there stands a leaky tap
drip
drip
drip

long lines of ants march through the moist earth

flies   through   droplets
     flit   the

the drips and drops
become a puddle

             beaks
       long
     their
   dip
birds
   into
     the
       murky
           water

the puddle
turns into a bog

```
g   g   g
r   r   r
e   a   o
e   s   w
n   s   s
```

wallabies   bound   over   to   nibble   the   new
  shoots

the bog expands
into a swamp

during the night   croak   frogs move in   croak   and
  claim the swamp   croak croak

the plumber sent to fix the leak
marvels at the wealth of life
and leaves the tap
d
r
i
p
p
i
n
g

Belonging

I long to be a tree
in an old growth forest,
roots growing deep
within my community.
But would I be content –
a faceless one of many?
Or do I need to be
the tree that makes the headlines
when the activist chains herself
to me?

Well Past Midnight

'Tis the witching hour of night,
Orbed is the moon and bright,
And the stars they glisten, glisten,
Seeming with bright eyes to listen –
For what listen they?

– John Keats

Wading

On lonely nights I wait for sleep to come,
time swims on by without a sideways glance.
My mind wades through the words I have become.

The words beat through my head like it's a drum,
my blood joins in, its path becomes a dance.
On lonely nights I wait for sleep to come.

My body's still, extremities are numb,
my toes and hands find slumber in advance.
My mind wades through the words I have become.

Wind beckons from the rooftops with its strum,
Come out with me, we'll pirouette and prance.
On lonely nights I wait for sleep to come.

If only time could end, its course be swum,
my thoughts would stop if given this one chance.
My mind wades through the words I have become.

I'm jealous of my husband's restful hum,
I long to join him in his pleasant trance.
On lonely nights I wait for sleep to come.
My mind wades through the words I have become.

My mind swims through clouds and
                 breaks into the sunlit void,
s c a t t e r i n g
           into   r
                       a
                       i
                       n
                       b
                       o
                       w
                       s
   before
       gravity
               takes hold. It cascades
                       down
                       down
                       down
       to oceans bleak. Sticky tendrils clasp it
                     pull it under.

Gasping, it shakes   free,
           swims   up   from the depths
     drags itself onto the beach
            and lies panting in the feeble sun.

Until it's caught in a fit of wind
and blown to   the land's far reaches.

        All the while,
        I brace my feet,
   entwine my fingers through its membranes
      and try to hold it steady.

A Bark of Thunder

A bark of thunder shudders
me awake, pulls me
from that halfway world
of fleeing thoughts and dreams.

Through the noise of silence
I strain to hear
the consequential rain
on road and roof.

My effort banishes
thoughts and dreams.
Sleep is but a distant hope.
If only it would rain more loudly.

Traitorous Eyes

You roll over for what must be the…
but you're not keeping count. That would definitely
chase away the longed for sleep.

As your arm slips under the pillow
and your foot finds a cool patch of sheet
your eyes slide to the bedside clock.

1:11

Numerical alliteration.
But you let it go because sleep is the aim,
not poetry.

You turn onto your back, adjust
your body into a straight line, arms slightly apart, palms up,
as your yoga teacher intones. And your mind floats.

Then, as sleep approaches, you roll to your right,
untangle your limbs from the cloying sheets
and those traitorous eyes torment you again.

2:22

The numbers cling to the corners of your consciousness.
With a sigh of resignation,
you creep from your bed,

fumble on the bedside table for your novel
and slink into the lounge, where beneath the gentle lamp
you slowly fill your mind with words.

Sated, you return to your bed
but your eyes turn instinctively
to the yellow numbers.

3:33

And with that third act of uncalled-for repetition
you realise that sleep
is but a dream.

In the Back of Emily Dickinson

Well past midnight
the pain cranks up a notch.
Through my tears I'm at a loss.
In desperation

wake my husband.
Sorry, Love, but I'm in pain.
Sleeping voice recommends ambulance.
Surely not.

Dial number for advice.
Sorry, it's not an emergency, it's just pain.
She questions through my apologies
and they're on their way, just like that.

He, sensible as ever,
helps me pack a bag
clothes for the morning, a toothbrush.
I throw in a book of poetry.

In the ambulance Sam
offers green inhaler to take the edge off,
may make your head spin though
and before long it does both.

But by then I'm there,
still clutching green magic,
and no-nonsense nurse Fiona says
I think you've had enough of that.

Reluctantly I relinquish it,
accept the offered white tablet.
Nurse struggles to take my blood pressure
and my head spins.

Then words pour in
to replace the pain
and I must capture them
before they escape.

She ignores my request for paper.
Maybe she just forgot
or maybe it's as she said,
I'd hate to see what you'd write about this place.

So I scribble this down
in the back of my book
of poetry.
Sorry, Emily.

His Hand

and so
her life as it once was
is all but gone

the tears
that beg to be released
remain unshed

her mind
full of the naked pain
is frozen, numb

his hand
once sweet with its caress
has left its mark

A(n end of) Love Sonnet

As crimson bruises blossom on my cheek
my husband guns our car into the night.
I screamed at him to leave, within a week
he'll crawl back home, beg pardon for the fight.

From in her room our treasured daughter cries;
instinctively I dim the lights with shame.
Or is it pride? Or fear of judging eyes?
Too many people think I share the blame.

The door creaks and her trusting eyes meet mine.
She smiles and pads softly to my side.
My love for her torpedoes up my spine
to banish thoughts of fear and shame and pride.

I hold her and I understand it well:
tonight my marriage ends. It's time to tell.

Sleeping Rough

We met one freezing morning at the park
and chatted while he warmed his cold behind
atop the park's free barbecue; a spark
ignited in my young son's budding mind.

He told us frankly he'd been sleeping rough;
my senses had already let me know.
He said he loved the great outdoors enough
to never need an indoor place to go.

But everybody needs a house to live,
my son declared, his solemn eyes lit up.
You're smart, my boy, the man said, *that I give.
What job will you do when you've grown up?*

His answer flushed me with a warmth right through:
A builder, and I'll build a house for you.

The Shed

With
sleepless rage
he left his bed and stomped
out to his neighbour's shed. Its vast expanse
of painted steel, a vex with which he could not deal.
He stood and glared upon its form, his body still, his mind a storm.
The air grew cold, dark gathered round, the wash of waves the only sound. With reason blurred by ageing night, a plan arose like clear moonlight: a plan based on the likelihood that shed's contents were made of wood. A match or two, a slender stick, a fuel soaked rag to make a wick. A narrow gap beside the door, insert the stick, and nothing more. He stood again in dark of night, anticipating his new sight. His heart rejoiced at crackles near, each fiery roar, to him a cheer. The orange glow, the blackened air, the growing heat: his answered prayer. A door banged shut. He turned his head. Someone approached; he filled with dread. But as the glow lit up her face, his fear dissolved without trace. It was his other neighbour, Sue: the ugly shed blocked her view too.

The Four of Us

Do you remember that evening,
so many moons ago,
when we built a bonfire on the beach,
back when the council permitted such things,
and roasted marshmallows,
which burnt,
but biting through the carbon shell we found melted sweetness?

And do you remember when I said we should go back to the house,
because even though it was summer it wasn't warm,
one of you replied,
No, let's wait until the moon rises?

Do you remember how we stayed
and told jokes
and made up tales about the builders of the other beach bonfires
and their imagined devious plans,
which made us laugh;
even more than the jokes,
so much that our faces hurt?

Do you remember how we waited until the fire burnt low,
until just the red coals remained
which we doused in sea water then buried deep in the soft sand,
because despite our silly tales we were sensible at heart?

And do you remember how,
when we trudged over the sand dunes,
we spotted the moon,
hours above the horizon?

But did you know
that evening has stayed in my memory
all these years?

And did you know I am forever thankful
for that sand dune hiding the moon
so that I could form this precious memory of
the four of us?

The Power of a Pen

dark
curled up in my bed
thoughts
gallop through my head
worries
clamour for attention
stress
weighs me down with tension
rise
squint in bedside light
pen
urges me to write
paper
cover with my scrawl
words
organise it all

dark
curled up in my bed
dreams
trickle through my head

Jealousy

Whenever
thunder rumbled
and lightning ripped the night
our long-haired cat
scrambled into our bedroom
slipped across the floorboards
leapt onto the bed
and burrowed under the blankets
to lie
safe and snug
curled up against
my sister.

My Dearest Love

Come to me, my dearest love
and wrap me in your gentle arms.
Hold me tight against your breast
to keep me safe from all life's harms.

Stroke me softly with your words,
whispered through my darkest hour.
Paint with them a land of peace,
a joyful life, a world in flower.

Hold me in each vengeful storm,
through anxious bursts and trails of woe.
Ease me with your endless strength.
Return me to that calm I know.

Of all my lovers in this life,
it's you that I will always keep.
It's you I yearn for every night.
It's you I love, my dearest Sleep.

I slip

into that delicious space
between wakefulness and sleep

drift on beams of lucid thought
dancing through clouds of dreams.

The jigsaw pieces of my day
dissolve around the edges

then fit together seamlessly
in ephemeral perfection.

Waves of Grief

I can wade grief,
Whole pools of it

– Emily Dickinson

Snowflakes on Your Coffin

That year
spring came early.
The almonds blossomed white against the bleak
then fell, like snowflakes,
as did you,
and all I knew was winter.
I could not see the ripening kernels
nor hear the screech of lorikeets come to feast.
I barely felt the stir of warmth.
But as the last leaf fell,
returning branches to the bleak,
our child was born
and I knew spring.

The Night Before Her Funeral

The storm pulled
me from a dreamless sleep. I lay
still with tension's heavy hand across my shoulders and listened
to the wind shout and rage and the rain hurl
its tears upon my roof, and I saw
that nothing in the world was at peace
which was exactly how it should be.

After

The day had been nicer than she'd expected –
conversations with old friends,
more hugs than tears,
she even got to see the Norwegian wedding photos.
It was only after the wake
as she trundled off to old routines
that the weight settled back across her shoulders
and the half-forgotten niggle in her stomach
metamorphosed into the taipan
that would stay, clamped on her intestines, to ensure
that the trivialities of her days would never
distract her from her task
of remembering.

You Think

You think you're doing fine.
You've dealt with life's latest distresses,
whether by talking them through with whoever will listen,
or reflecting on them at great length in private,
whichever is your preference at the time,
and they are now safely filed away in the big steel-grey filing cabinet of your mind.

Then one day,
say while you are washing the dishes,
standing at the sink with your hands in the luke-warm water
patiently, or perhaps not so patiently,
scraping hardened pieces of pasta out of the bottom of an already scratched saucepan,
maybe watching the swallows that are nesting in the carport fly in front of the kitchen window,

without warning
one of your filed distresses jumps on a motorbike,
leaps the wall of the cabinet
and slams full speed into your consciousness,
leaving you standing motionless with a dirty pot in your hands
that you are no longer remotely capable of dealing with.

Grandma's Grey Goggles

I was eight when Grandma died.
I cried, but not as much as Mum.
At the funeral she wiped her eyes and wrapped her arms around me tight.
We'll always miss Grandma, she whispered,
but every time we think of her she'll be there,
with us, in our minds.

A few weeks later Mum went to Grandpa's
and brought home a cardboard box.
Memories danced while we unwrapped the treasures:
Grandma's scarlet vest, her silver broach from Norway,
the last scarf she knitted
and her grey goggles.

I've never had goggles, Mum said.
Now I can swim under water with you.
I remember how, that weekend, we raced the length of Auntie Jane's pool.
Mum and I laughed out loud when we reached the end,
our hands slapping the tiles together.
It felt so good to see Mum happy again.

When we headed north for our ten-week holiday
– a whole term off school! –
Mum took Grandma's goggles with her.
I have a photo of her, beneath the waterfall, her face in the water.
Wow! Look at all the fish down there! she cried.
In my rush to join her, I yanked too hard, and my goggle strap snapped.

Never mind, my darling.
You can have Grandma's, Mum said.
I could have refused, said,
no, they're yours now, but I was only eight.
So I dived under the water and thought of Grandma.
She'd loved to swim too.

At the next caravan park I made a new friend.
We raced across the pool. I was sure my goggles helped me win.
I imagined Grandma saying,
Well done, I'm so proud of you! like she always did.
Afterwards, when I towelled myself dry,
I thought of Grandma's arms hugging me tight.

At the rock pools
Mum, Dad and I did bombs into the deep water.
I set the goggles on a boulder so they wouldn't get lost.
After each bomb I checked they were safe.
The goggles stared back at me
and it seemed as though Grandma was watching me too.

By the time we got home
Grandma's goggles had been to
eight swimming pools, six waterfalls,
three rivers and four different rock pools
all the way across Australia.
And each place I thought of Grandma.

Now, all these years later,
when I think back on our trip
and remember those wonderful adventures
with my mum and dad,
I also think of Grandma.
It's almost like she went on our holiday with us.

Waves of Grief

The waves of grief wash in, wash out,
and so my life is tossed about
with days of pain and anxious fears,
wide fields of calm, then gusts of tears.

The journey of my grief is vast:
it weaves its tendrils through my past
and stretches far as I can see,
an endless sensibility.

But grief is how I keep her near
and so I do not live in fear
of grief's waves crashing on my shore.
I brace myself and wait for more.

Today

I saw you today,
as I drove home alone.
You were standing beside the road,
waiting to cross.
You wore your crimson vest,
the one I've long coveted,
and your grey hair was cut short.
It suited you.
But before I could wave hello
I remembered that it was not you,
could never be you,
and that your crimson vest is now mine.

Left Baggage

I left some baggage with a friend.
I don't know what's become of it,
she's never mentioned it again.

She welcomed it as it arrived,
that leaden, jumbled mess of words.
She didn't judge or criticise.

Just gently stowed it out of sight
in no one's way or train of thought.
I guess it's there still, locked away.

Last Night

Last night
I hugged my mum.
She hugged me back,
tight.

I breathed her scent
of washing powder
and knew that I was safe
and loved.

I whispered
in her soft grey hair
I'm so glad you didn't die
and then I woke.

She Paints the Sky

she paints

   mashed potato clouds
scraped across a Wedgwood plate

   her grandmother's curls,
        kitten grey and powder white,
  without a trace of that awful rinse

she paints

   the early April sunset that turned the world
       an improbable pink

      and the late winter dawn
  where her juice jumped onto the horizon

and with her oils mixed
just so

she paints

   the most satisfying
    block of blue

when the stresses
      of her days on earth
   press between her shoulders

she gazes up
      and paints the sky.

Simple

It was not the sun's warm invitation
nor the baby-blanket blue sky
that drew me out of the house on that early autumn day
but the chore of pegging up washing,
or heaping dry clothes in the basket,
I do not recall which.
Nor do I recall why I paused
and glanced up.
Did I hear the wings flapping?
Or feel the movement of the displaced air?
Surely not. The bird, while hovering directly above,
was at too great a height, that of the canopy of a hundred-year gum.
But I remember the piano-key wings of the common garden magpie
moving furiously against the immense blue backdrop
while all else stilled and was forgotten.
And I have promised myself that I will always remember
how at that moment I felt
simply happy.

Acknowledgements

There are many people who have been involved in creating this collection. I thank you all immensely.

Firstly, thank you to all the people whose stories have inspired my poems; I have pilfered moments from family, friends' and complete strangers' lives to weave into my poetry, and intertwined them with threads from my imagination to create these little works of fiction.

Next, a huge thank you to everyone in my writers' group for your support and editing brilliance: Lynette Washington, Tom Di Santo, Alys Jackson, Elaine Cain, Louise Friebe, Michele Fairbairn, Nicola McGunnigle and Kimberley Zeneth; writing wouldn't be nearly as much fun without you.

Thank you to Friendly Street Poets for a wonderfully supportive poetry community and for the opportunity to be published in your beautiful anthologies. In particular thank you to Lilliana Rose, Louise McKenna and Glen Johns for your editing suggestions, and to Judy Dally for inspiring me to put this collection together and submit it to Ginninderra Press.

Thanks to the SA Writers' Centre for helping me develop as a writer, to Jude Aquilina for your advice, and to Tracey Davis and the Open Your Mind poetry competition for helping me realise that I am a poet.

Thank you to Stephen Mathews and Ginninderra Press for publishing *Paint the Sky* and enabling my dream to come true.

Thanks Dad for letting me give you copies of every poem I've had published, and for reading them and being proud of me. You can add this book to your collection.

And thank you so much David, Che and Matt for your love.

Finally, thank you to all the anthologies, magazines, websites and art exhibitions that have previously published poems that appear in *Paint the Sky*:

Sorcerers and Soothsayers, Friendly Street Poets 35 (2011) for 'Snowflakes on your Coffin';

Flying Kites, Friendly Street Poets 36 (2012) for 'Time and Space';

Patterns of Living, Friendly Street Poets 37 (2013) for 'After';

The Infinite Dirt, Friendly Street Poets 38 (2014) for 'Whistling Kites';

Silver Singing Streams, Friendly Street Poets 39 (2015) for 'She Paints the Sky' and 'I Thought I Knew Her';

Many Eyes, Many Voices, Friendly Street Poets 40 (2016) for 'Last Night' and 'A(n end of) Love Sonnet';

Bimblebox 153 Birds Art Project for 'Whistling Kites';

Blast Off (The School Magazine) for 'The Leaky Tap Swamp';

Countdown (The School Magazine) for 'A Walk by the Sea';

In Daily for 'The Threat of Genetics', 'Simple' and 'I Thought I Knew Her';

The Mozzie for 'His Hand', 'Belonging', 'The Waves', 'My Mind', 'A Bark of Thunder', 'Till Death Do Us', 'Six Times Round the Sun', 'The Night Before her Funeral', 'His Lament', 'Caress' (published as 'Tide'), 'Mary at 96', 'Today', 'Beyond the Dingo Fence' (published as 'The Dingo's Bed'), 'It's Work' and 'You Think';

Orbit (The School Magazine) for 'The Catch of the Evening';

Parenting Express for 'Darling';

Poetrix for 'Wading';

Positive Words for earlier versions of 'Sweetest Failure', 'The Power of a Pen' (published as 'The Power of Pen and Paper'), 'My Dearest Love' and 'The Shed';

Valley Micropress for 'A Bark of Thunder'.

www.ingramcontent.com/pod-product-compliance
Lightning Source LLC
Chambersburg PA
CBHW062148100526
44589CB00014B/1738